EMMANUEL JOSEPH

The Unwritten Constellation, Mapping Your Path Through Chaos, Courage, and Clarity

Copyright © 2025 by Emmanuel Joseph

All rights reserved. No part of this publication may be reproduced, stored or transmitted in any form or by any means, electronic, mechanical, photocopying, recording, scanning, or otherwise without written permission from the publisher. It is illegal to copy this book, post it to a website, or distribute it by any other means without permission.

First edition

This book was professionally typeset on Reedsy. Find out more at reedsy.com

Contents

1	Chapter 1: The Cosmic Beginning	1
2	Chapter 2: Embracing the Unknown	3
3	Chapter 3: The Power of Choice	5
4	Chapter 4: Navigating Chaos	7
5	Chapter 5: The Courage to Change	9
6	Chapter 6: Finding Clarity	11
7	Chapter 6: Finding Clarity	12
8	Chapter 7: Building Resilience	13
9	Chapter 8: The Art of Letting Go	15
10	Chapter 9: Cultivating Inner Peace	17
11	Chapter 10: Embracing Vulnerability	19
12	Chapter 11: The Importance of Gratitude	21
13	Chapter 12: The Power of Mindfulness	23
14	Chapter 13: The Journey of Self-Discovery	25
15	Chapter 14: Embracing Change	27
16	Chapter 15: The Power of Intention	28
17	Chapter 16: The Journey of Self-Acceptance	29
18	Chapter 17: Mapping Your Path	30

1

Chapter 1: The Cosmic Beginning

From the dawn of time, the universe has been a vast expanse of mystery and wonder. Imagine standing on the precipice of existence, gazing into the infinite tapestry of stars. Each twinkling light represents a story, an untold journey, a path yet to be discovered. The cosmos is a metaphor for our own lives, filled with chaos, courage, and clarity. As we embark on this journey through the unwritten constellation, we must understand that our paths are not predefined but are crafted by our choices, dreams, and actions.

As we navigate the chaotic universe, we encounter countless obstacles and uncertainties. These challenges are not meant to deter us but to strengthen our resolve and ignite our courage. It is in the face of adversity that we discover our true potential. Just as stars are born from the collapse of cosmic clouds, we too can emerge stronger and brighter from the trials we face. Embracing chaos is the first step in mapping our path through the constellation.

Courage is the beacon that guides us through the darkness. It is the force that propels us forward when the night is at its darkest. Courage is not the absence of fear, but the triumph over it. It is the inner strength that allows us to take risks, to venture into the unknown, and to trust in our ability to overcome. As we journey through the constellation, we must cultivate courage and let it illuminate our path.

THE UNWRITTEN CONSTELLATION, MAPPING YOUR PATH THROUGH CHAOS, COURAGE, AND CLARITY

Clarity is the destination we seek. It is the moment when the chaos subsides, and the stars align to reveal our true purpose. Clarity is not a state of constant certainty but a fleeting glimpse of understanding that guides our actions. It is the realization that our path is not a straight line but a series of interconnected steps that lead us closer to our dreams. As we navigate the unwritten constellation, we must strive for clarity, knowing that it will light our way through the darkest nights.

2

Chapter 2: Embracing the Unknown

Life is an unpredictable journey, and the unknown is an integral part of our existence. Embracing the unknown requires a willingness to step out of our comfort zones and explore uncharted territories. It is in these moments of uncertainty that we discover our true selves. The unknown is not something to be feared but an opportunity for growth and self-discovery. By embracing the unknown, we open ourselves up to new experiences, perspectives, and possibilities.

When we embrace the unknown, we allow ourselves to be vulnerable. Vulnerability is often seen as a weakness, but it is, in fact, a source of strength. It is the courage to be imperfect, to take risks, and to face the possibility of failure. Embracing vulnerability allows us to connect with others on a deeper level and to build meaningful relationships. It is through vulnerability that we find our greatest strength and resilience.

The unknown is also a catalyst for innovation and creativity. When we venture into uncharted territories, we are forced to think outside the box and come up with new solutions to old problems. Embracing the unknown encourages us to be curious, to ask questions, and to challenge the status quo. It is through this process of exploration and experimentation that we discover new ideas, opportunities, and paths.

Ultimately, embracing the unknown is about trusting the journey. It is about having faith in ourselves and our ability to navigate the twists and turns of life. It is about recognizing that the journey is just as important as the destination. By embracing the unknown, we learn to appreciate the beauty of the journey and to find joy in the unexpected. It is through this process of exploration and discovery that we map our path through the unwritten constellation.

3

Chapter 3: The Power of Choice

Our lives are defined by the choices we make. Every decision, no matter how small, has the power to shape our future. The power of choice is a gift that allows us to take control of our destiny and to create the life we desire. By recognizing the power of choice, we can make deliberate and intentional decisions that align with our values and aspirations.

Making choices requires self-awareness and reflection. It is important to understand our motivations, desires, and goals. By taking the time to reflect on what truly matters to us, we can make choices that are authentic and meaningful. Self-awareness allows us to recognize when we are making choices out of fear, habit, or external pressure, and to instead make choices that are true to ourselves.

The power of choice also comes with responsibility. We must take ownership of our decisions and be accountable for the consequences. It is easy to blame others or external circumstances for our challenges, but true empowerment comes from recognizing that we are in control of our destiny. By taking responsibility for our choices, we can learn from our mistakes, grow from our experiences, and build a life that reflects our true potential.

Ultimately, the power of choice is about creating a life of purpose and fulfillment. It is about making decisions that align with our values, passions, and goals. It is about recognizing that we have the ability to shape our own path and to create a life that is meaningful and fulfilling. By embracing the power of choice, we can map our path through the unwritten constellation and navigate the chaos, courage, and clarity that define our journey.

4

Chapter 4: Navigating Chaos

Chaos is an inevitable part of life. It is the storm that disrupts our plans, the unexpected twist that throws us off course. But chaos is not something to be feared; it is an opportunity for growth and transformation. Navigating chaos requires resilience, adaptability, and a positive mindset. It is through the process of navigating chaos that we discover our true strength and potential.

Resilience is the ability to bounce back from adversity and to keep moving forward despite challenges. It is the inner strength that allows us to persevere in the face of hardship. Resilience is not something we are born with; it is a skill that we can develop through practice and experience. By cultivating resilience, we can navigate the chaos of life with grace and determination.

Adaptability is the ability to adjust to new situations and to embrace change. It is the flexibility to pivot and to find new solutions when our plans are disrupted. Adaptability requires an open mind and a willingness to let go of our preconceived notions and expectations. By embracing adaptability, we can navigate the chaos of life with creativity and resourcefulness.

A positive mindset is essential for navigating chaos. It is the ability to find the silver lining in every situation and to focus on the opportunities rather than the obstacles. A positive mindset allows us to stay motivated and to maintain a sense of hope and optimism, even in the face of adversity. By cultivating a positive mindset, we can navigate the chaos of life with resilience and determination.

Ultimately, navigating chaos is about finding balance and harmony amidst the turbulence. It is about recognizing that chaos is a natural part of life and that it can be a catalyst for growth and transformation. By embracing chaos, we can navigate the unwritten constellation with courage and clarity, and discover our true potential.

5

Chapter 5: The Courage to Change

Change is a constant in life, and it requires courage to embrace it. The courage to change is the willingness to let go of the familiar and to step into the unknown. It is the bravery to face our fears, to take risks, and to trust in our ability to adapt and grow. The courage to change is not about being fearless; it is about acknowledging our fears and moving forward despite them.

Change often brings uncertainty and discomfort. It is natural to feel resistance and to cling to the familiar. But it is through the process of change that we discover new possibilities and opportunities. The courage to change requires us to step out of our comfort zones and to embrace the unknown. It is through this process of exploration and growth that we find our true potential.

The courage to change also requires us to let go of the past. It is about releasing old habits, beliefs, and patterns that no longer serve us. Letting go is not about forgetting or dismissing the past; it is about acknowledging its impact and choosing to move forward. By letting go of the past, we create space for new experiences, perspectives, and opportunities.

Ultimately, the courage to change is about trusting the process. It is about having faith in ourselves and our ability to navigate the twists and turns of life. It is about recognizing that change is not something to be feared, but an opportunity for growth and transformation. By embracing the courage to change, we can map our path through the unwritten constellation and discover new horizons.

6

Chapter 6: Finding Clarity

Clarity is the key to navigating the chaos of life. It is the ability to see things clearly and to understand our true purpose and direction. Finding clarity requires self-reflection, mindfulness, and a willingness to explore our inner landscape. It is through this process of self-discovery that we gain insight and wisdom, and find the clarity we seek.

Self-reflection is the process of looking inward and examining our thoughts, feelings, and actions. It is about understanding our motivations, desires, and goals. By taking the time to reflect on our experiences, we gain a deeper understanding of ourselves and our path. Self-reflection allows us to identify our strengths and weaknesses, and to make intentional choices that align with our true purpose.

Mindfulness is the practice of being present in the moment and paying attention to our thoughts and feelings without judgment. It is about cultivating awareness and acceptance of our inner experiences. Mindfulness allows us to quiet the noise of the outside world and to connect with our inner wisdom. By practicing mindfulness, we can find clarity and insight, and navigate the chaos of life with grace and ease.

7

Chapter 6: Finding Clarity

Exploring our inner landscape requires us to be curious and open-minded. It is about asking questions, seeking answers, and being willing to challenge our assumptions. By exploring our inner world, we gain insight into our true selves and our deepest desires. This process of self-exploration allows us to uncover our strengths, passions, and purpose, and to find clarity in our path.

Finding clarity also involves setting intentions and goals. It is about defining what we want to achieve and creating a roadmap to get there. Setting clear intentions allows us to focus our energy and efforts on what truly matters. It is important to set realistic and achievable goals, and to break them down into smaller, manageable steps. By setting intentions and goals, we can create a sense of direction and purpose, and navigate the chaos of life with clarity and confidence.

Clarity is not a one-time achievement; it is an ongoing process. It requires continuous self-reflection, mindfulness, and exploration. As we grow and evolve, our path may change, and our goals may shift. It is important to remain flexible and open to new possibilities. By embracing the journey of finding clarity, we can navigate the unwritten constellation with grace and ease, and discover our true purpose and potential.

8

Chapter 7: Building Resilience

Resilience is the ability to bounce back from adversity and to keep moving forward despite challenges. It is the inner strength that allows us to persevere in the face of hardship. Building resilience requires us to cultivate a positive mindset, develop coping strategies, and find support from others. It is through the process of building resilience that we discover our true strength and potential.

Cultivating a positive mindset is essential for building resilience. It is about focusing on the opportunities rather than the obstacles, and finding the silver lining in every situation. A positive mindset allows us to stay motivated and to maintain a sense of hope and optimism, even in the face of adversity. By practicing gratitude, mindfulness, and positive thinking, we can cultivate a positive mindset and build resilience.

Developing coping strategies is also important for building resilience. It is about finding healthy ways to manage stress, emotions, and challenges. Coping strategies can include physical activities, such as exercise and yoga, as well as mental and emotional practices, such as meditation, journaling, and seeking support from others. By developing coping strategies, we can navigate the ups and downs of life with resilience and determination.

Finding support from others is crucial for building resilience. It is about building a network of family, friends, and mentors who can provide encouragement, guidance, and support. It is important to reach out for help when needed and to surround ourselves with positive and supportive people. By finding support from others, we can build resilience and navigate the challenges of life with strength and grace.

9

Chapter 8: The Art of Letting Go

Letting go is an essential part of the journey through the unwritten constellation. It is about releasing old habits, beliefs, and patterns that no longer serve us. Letting go is not about forgetting or dismissing the past; it is about acknowledging its impact and choosing to move forward. By letting go, we create space for new experiences, perspectives, and opportunities.

Letting go requires acceptance and forgiveness. It is about accepting the things we cannot change and forgiving ourselves and others for past mistakes. Acceptance allows us to find peace and to move forward with grace and ease. Forgiveness allows us to release resentment and to find healing and growth. By practicing acceptance and forgiveness, we can let go of the past and create a brighter future.

Letting go also involves releasing control and surrendering to the flow of life. It is about trusting the journey and having faith in ourselves and the universe. Surrendering does not mean giving up; it means letting go of our need to control every aspect of our lives and allowing things to unfold naturally. By releasing control and surrendering to the flow of life, we can find freedom and joy in the present moment.

Ultimately, letting go is about creating space for new beginnings. It is about recognizing that the past does not define us and that we have the power to create a new future. By letting go, we can release old patterns and beliefs that hold us back and embrace new opportunities and possibilities. It is through the process of letting go that we can navigate the unwritten constellation with courage and clarity, and discover our true potential.

10

Chapter 9: Cultivating Inner Peace

Inner peace is the foundation for navigating the chaos of life. It is the sense of calm and tranquility that comes from within, regardless of external circumstances. Cultivating inner peace requires mindfulness, self-care, and a positive mindset. It is through the process of cultivating inner peace that we find balance and harmony in our lives.

Mindfulness is the practice of being present in the moment and paying attention to our thoughts and feelings without judgment. It is about cultivating awareness and acceptance of our inner experiences. Mindfulness allows us to quiet the noise of the outside world and to connect with our inner wisdom. By practicing mindfulness, we can find inner peace and navigate the chaos of life with grace and ease.

Self-care is also essential for cultivating inner peace. It is about taking care of our physical, mental, and emotional well-being. Self-care can include activities such as exercise, healthy eating, rest, and relaxation, as well as practices such as meditation, journaling, and spending time in nature. By prioritizing self-care, we can nurture our inner peace and build a strong foundation for navigating life's challenges.

A positive mindset is crucial for cultivating inner peace. It is about focusing on the positive aspects of life and finding joy in the present moment. A positive mindset allows us to stay motivated and to maintain a sense of hope and optimism, even in the face of adversity. By practicing gratitude, positive thinking, and self-compassion, we can cultivate a positive mindset and find inner peace.

Ultimately, cultivating inner peace is about finding balance and harmony within ourselves. It is about recognizing that we have the power to create our own sense of peace and tranquility, regardless of external circumstances. By cultivating inner peace, we can navigate the unwritten constellation with courage and clarity, and discover our true potential.

11

Chapter 10: Embracing Vulnerability

Vulnerability is often seen as a weakness, but it is, in fact, a source of strength. Embracing vulnerability requires us to be open and honest about our true selves, to take risks, and to face the possibility of failure. It is through the process of embracing vulnerability that we build deeper connections with others and discover our true potential.

Embracing vulnerability involves being authentic and true to ourselves. It is about letting go of the need to be perfect and allowing ourselves to be seen for who we truly are. Authenticity allows us to build meaningful relationships and to connect with others on a deeper level. By being open and honest about our thoughts, feelings, and experiences, we create a space for genuine connection and understanding.

Taking risks is also an important part of embracing vulnerability. It is about stepping out of our comfort zones and challenging ourselves to try new things. Taking risks requires courage and the willingness to face the possibility of failure. But it is through taking risks that we grow, learn, and discover new possibilities. By embracing vulnerability and taking risks, we can navigate the chaos of life with courage and determination.

Facing the possibility of failure is another aspect of embracing vulnerability. It is about recognizing that failure is not a reflection of our worth, but a part of the learning process. Failure is an opportunity to learn, grow, and improve. By embracing vulnerability and facing the possibility of failure, we can build resilience and discover our true strength.

12

Chapter 11: The Importance of Gratitude

Gratitude is a powerful tool for navigating the chaos of life. It is the practice of focusing on the positive aspects of our lives and appreciating the good things we have. Cultivating gratitude allows us to find joy and contentment in the present moment and to build a positive mindset.

Gratitude involves recognizing and appreciating the small things in life. It is about finding joy in the simple pleasures and moments of beauty that surround us every day. By focusing on the positive aspects of our lives, we can shift our perspective and find happiness in the present moment.

Practicing gratitude also involves expressing appreciation for the people in our lives. It is about acknowledging the support, kindness, and love we receive from others and showing our appreciation. By expressing gratitude, we can build stronger relationships and create a positive and supportive environment.

Gratitude is also a tool for building resilience. It allows us to focus on the positive aspects of our lives, even in the face of challenges and adversity. By practicing gratitude, we can find strength and hope in difficult times and navigate the chaos of life with grace and determination.

Ultimately, gratitude is about finding contentment and joy in the present moment. It is about recognizing the good things we have and appreciating the beauty of life. By cultivating gratitude, we can navigate the unwritten constellation with a positive mindset and discover our true potential.

13

Chapter 12: The Power of Mindfulness

Mindfulness is the practice of being present in the moment and paying attention to our thoughts and feelings without judgment. It is a powerful tool for navigating the chaos of life and finding clarity and peace. By practicing mindfulness, we can cultivate awareness and acceptance of our inner experiences and build a strong foundation for navigating life's challenges.

Mindfulness involves paying attention to our thoughts and feelings in a non-judgmental way. It is about observing our inner experiences with curiosity and acceptance. By practicing mindfulness, we can gain insight into our thoughts and emotions and develop a deeper understanding of ourselves.

Mindfulness also involves being present in the moment. It is about focusing our attention on the here and now, rather than worrying about the past or the future. By being present in the moment, we can find peace and clarity and fully experience the richness of life.

Practicing mindfulness can also help us manage stress and emotions. It allows us to stay grounded and centered in the face of challenges and adversity. By practicing mindfulness, we can build resilience and navigate the chaos of life with grace and ease.

Ultimately, mindfulness is about cultivating a sense of awareness and acceptance of our inner experiences. It is about finding peace and clarity in the present moment and building a strong foundation for navigating life's challenges. By practicing mindfulness, we can navigate the unwritten constellation with courage and clarity and discover our true potential.

14

Chapter 13: The Journey of Self-Discovery

Self-discovery is a lifelong journey of exploring our inner world and uncovering our true selves. It is the process of understanding our motivations, desires, and goals, and finding our true purpose and path. The journey of self-discovery requires curiosity, openness, and a willingness to explore our inner landscape.

The journey of self-discovery involves asking questions and seeking answers. It is about being curious and open-minded, and exploring our thoughts, feelings, and experiences. By asking questions and seeking answers, we can gain insight into our true selves and uncover our strengths, passions, and purpose.

Self-discovery also involves reflection and introspection. It is about taking the time to reflect on our experiences and to understand our inner world. Reflection allows us to gain a deeper understanding of ourselves and our path and to make intentional choices that align with our true purpose.

The journey of self-discovery is also about embracing change and growth. It is about recognizing that we are constantly evolving and that our path may change over time. By embracing change and growth, we can continue to explore our inner world and discover new possibilities and opportunities.

Ultimately, the journey of self-discovery is about finding our true selves and our true purpose. It is about understanding our motivations, desires, and goals, and creating a life that reflects our true potential. By embarking on the journey of self-discovery, we can navigate the unwritten constellation with courage and clarity and discover our true potential.

15

Chapter 14: Embracing Change

C hange is an inevitable part of life. It is the force that drives growth and transformation. Embracing change requires us to be adaptable, open-minded, and willing to let go of the familiar. It is through the process of embracing change that we discover new possibilities and opportunities.

Embracing change involves being open to new experiences and perspectives. It is about being curious and willing to explore new ideas and possibilities. By embracing change, we can expand our horizons and discover new paths and opportunities.

Adapting to change is also important. It is about being flexible and willing to adjust our plans and expectations. Adaptability allows us to navigate the twists and turns of life with grace and ease. By being adaptable, we can find new solutions to old problems and discover new possibilities.

Letting go of the familiar is another aspect of embracing change. It is about releasing old habits, beliefs, and patterns that no longer serve us. Letting go allows us to create space for new experiences and opportunities. By embracing change and letting go of the familiar, we can navigate the chaos of life with courage and clarity.

16

Chapter 15: The Power of Intention

Intention is the driving force behind our actions and decisions. It is the purpose and motivation that guides our path. The power of intention lies in its ability to focus our energy and efforts on what truly matters. By setting clear intentions, we can create a sense of direction and purpose in our lives.

Setting intentions involves defining what we want to achieve and why it is important to us. It is about understanding our motivations and desires and aligning our actions with our true purpose. By setting clear intentions, we can focus our energy and efforts on what truly matters.

The power of intention also involves being deliberate and intentional in our actions. It is about making choices that align with our values and goals. By being intentional in our actions, we can create a sense of direction and purpose in our lives.

Ultimately, the power of intention is about creating a life of purpose and fulfillment. It is about setting clear intentions and taking deliberate actions that align with our true purpose. By harnessing the power of intention, we can navigate the unwritten constellation with courage and clarity and discover our true potential.

17

Chapter 16: The Journey of Self-Acceptance

Self-acceptance is the foundation for navigating the chaos of life. It is the process of embracing our true selves and accepting our strengths and weaknesses. The journey of self-acceptance requires compassion, forgiveness, and a willingness to let go of self-judgment.

Self-acceptance involves recognizing and embracing our strengths and weaknesses. It is about acknowledging our imperfections and accepting ourselves for who we truly are. By practicing self-acceptance, we can build a strong foundation for navigating life's challenges.

Forgiveness is also an important part of self-acceptance. It is about letting go of past mistakes and forgiving ourselves for our imperfections. Forgiveness allows us to find healing and growth and to move forward with grace and ease. By practicing forgiveness, we can embrace our true selves and find peace and contentment.

Ultimately, the journey of self-acceptance is about finding compassion and love for ourselves. It is about recognizing our worth and embracing our true potential. By embarking on the journey of self-acceptance, we can navigate the unwritten constellation with courage and clarity and discover our true potential.

18

Chapter 17: Mapping Your Path

Mapping your path is the final step in navigating the unwritten constellation. It is the process of creating a roadmap for your life and defining your true purpose and direction. Mapping your path requires self-reflection, goal-setting, and a willingness to embrace change.

Mapping your path involves reflecting on your experiences and understanding your true purpose and direction. It is about defining your values, passions, and goals and creating a roadmap to achieve them. By mapping your path, you can create a sense of direction and purpose in your life.

Goal-setting is also an important part of mapping your path. It is about defining what you want to achieve and creating a plan to get there. Goal-setting allows you to focus your energy and efforts on what truly matters and to create a sense of direction and purpose.

Embracing change is also important for mapping your path. It is about being adaptable and willing to adjust your plans and expectations. Embracing change allows you to navigate the twists and turns of life with grace and ease and to discover new possibilities and opportunities.

Ultimately, mapping your path is about creating a life of purpose and fulfillment. It is about defining your true purpose and direction and taking deliberate actions to achieve your goals. By mapping your path, you can navigate the unwritten constellation with courage and clarity and discover

CHAPTER 17: MAPPING YOUR PATH

your true potential.

In **"The Unwritten Constellation: Mapping Your Path Through Chaos, Courage, and Clarity,"** embark on a transformative journey through the vast and mysterious expanse of life. This inspiring guide takes you on a voyage through 17 compelling chapters, each designed to help you navigate the chaos, summon your courage, and find clarity in your path.

From embracing the unknown to cultivating inner peace, this book offers practical wisdom and profound insights to help you thrive in an unpredictable world. Learn to harness the power of choice, build resilience, and embrace change with confidence. Discover the art of letting go, the importance of gratitude, and the transformative power of mindfulness.

Through self-reflection and intention-setting, uncover your true purpose and create a life of meaning and fulfillment. With each chapter, you'll find the tools and inspiration you need to navigate the twists and turns of life with grace and determination.

"The Unwritten Constellation" is more than a guide—it's a companion on your journey to self-discovery and empowerment. Whether you're seeking direction, facing challenges, or simply looking to enrich your life, this book will illuminate your path and help you chart a course through the stars.

www.ingramcontent.com/pod-product-compliance
Lightning Source LLC
LaVergne TN
LVHW020739090526
838202LV00057BA/6134